Up to You!

A Self-Help Guide to Addiction Recovery

"It all begins with you!"

BY J. E. GRAVES

DORRANCE
PUBLISHING CO
EST. 1920
PITTSBURGH, PENNSYLVANIA 15238

Dorrance Publishing Co
585 Alpha Drive
Pittsburgh, PA 15238
Visit our website at www.dorrancebookstore.com

ISBN: 979-8-88812-088-0
eISBN: 979-8-88812-588-5

The King James Bible, KJV is public domain in the United States.

Up to You!

A Self-Help Guide to Addiction Recovery

"It all begins with you!"

To my wife and daughter.
Thank you for helping me believe in myself.

ACKNOWLEDGMENTS

I am eternally grateful to God, my family, friends, doctors, and my spiritual provider. They were there when I needed help the most. They helped me put my life in perspective when no one could. If it wasn't for them helping me, I know I would still be in that dark place that was slowly killing me.

"Believe in Yourself"

CONTENTS

INTRODUCTION

Deaths associated with alcohol, drugs, and suicide took the lives of 186,763 Americans in 2020, a 20 percent, one-year increase in the combined death rate and the highest number of substance misuse deaths ever recorded for a single year.[1]

I was so close to being a part of these statistics. I had to put up one heck of a fight to win the battle with my addiction. I thank God that I can now look back at my life and smile. Unfortunately, there are so many who cannot. I have lost friends and acquaintances over the years due to their addiction, and I am sure I will lose more. Folks, you can still take back your life. Tell yourself now, before things get worse, that you are not going to be among those statistics I just mentioned.

During my struggles with alcohol, I tried numerous times to quit. I was guided by my instincts, which failed me. I reached out so many times, begging for support groups, treatment centers, and hospitals to help me. Though they were all good, none of them could keep me from going back to my addiction. I had to figure out another way to stop drinking. I had to clear my mind from the distractions, get the demons tormenting me out of my head, and I had to avoid the temptations that were all around me.

While working on my recovery, I started writing down the things that were working for me. I would read them to myself, to others, and to my higher power, God. I do not expect everyone to agree with me or understand what I have written, but I do believe that those who have tried everything to no avail might just benefit from what I have put in this book. Believe me, it couldn't hurt!

**Think about where you are going,
not where you have been.**

PREFACE

Before I begin, I want to make it clear to everyone out there that I am not a doctor, counselor, therapist, or a theologian. I do not have a degree in medicine, counseling, or theology, nor will I ever claim to have one. I started journaling my experiences and the things that were working for me. They are not scientific or psychological observations of any kind. If I quoted another author or publication, I put a source with them.

You will notice throughout this book that there are Bible verses. These Bible verses helped me tremendously while I was working on my recovery. The Bible verses I used are from The King James Version (KJV). If you do not like this version, you can always look up the verses I used in your preferred Bible.

The basis of this book came about from my struggles with alcohol addiction and the numerous attempts and failures I had over the years. They are not perfect by far, but they are strategies and ideas that worked for me. They might work for you if you are serious and want to end your addiction, especially if you have tried other programs in the past with no success.

This is not a Twelve Step, secular, or Christian program; it is my program that worked for me. Please, do not misunderstand me on this, I believe in the Twelve Steps and other support group programs. I have been to several meetings over the years, but unfortunately, none of them worked for me. I found out that I needed more structure in my life; something that would take a hold of me and not let go. I had to open my mind to all possibilities that I had at my disposal.

Remember, these are just suggestions that might work if you put an effort into them. You have nothing to lose if you try. Also, if you disagree with some of my approaches, that is okay. Everyone is entitled to their own opinion. If you do not like what I have written, stop reading it. It obviously was not meant for you.

> But seek ye first the kingdom of God, and his right-
> eousness; and all these things shall be added unto you.
>
> Matthew 6:33
> King James Version (KJV)

Note: It does not matter what or who you believe in as long as you believe in YOURSELF. You are the answer to your recovery. I just happen to have God in my life. He helped me when I needed someone in my life other than my family and friends.

As I mentioned earlier, I used Bible verses throughout this book. If you are not into Bible verses, find someone or something else who will motivate you and keep you focused on your recovery.

Caution: Do not attempt to recover by yourself. It is too dangerous.

Did You Know?

- Almost 21 million Americans have at least one addiction, yet only 10 percent of them receive treatment.
- Drug overdose deaths have more than tripled since 1990.
- About 20 percent of Americans who have depression or an anxiety disorder also have a substance abuse disorder.
- More than 90 percent of people who have an addiction started to drink alcohol or use drugs before they were 18 years old.
- Every year, worldwide, alcohol is the cause of 5.3 percent of deaths (one in every 20).
- About 300 million people throughout the world have an alcohol use disorder.
- About 88,000 people die as a result of alcohol every year in the United States.
- About 130 Americans die every day from an opioid overdose.
- Approximately 2.1 million Americans have an opioid use disorder.
- About 30-40 million Americans smoke marijuana every year.
- Roughly 10 percent of all marijuana users will become addicted to the drug.
- About 34 million Americans smoke cigarettes.
- About 774,000 Americans are regular meth users. About 16,000 of them are between the ages of 12 and 17.
- Meth overdose fatalities increased almost threefold from 2015 to 2019.[2]

1
In the Beginning

Part 1

Watch and pray, that ye enter not into temptation: the
spirit indeed is willing, but the flesh is weak.

Matthew 26:41

As I sat in my third-floor apartment, I saw people out by the pool en-
joying themselves with others—and here I sat, alone, isolated, wallowing
in self-pity; what a terrible feeling to have about yourself. As I look back
on my life, I realized I put myself in this mess. I knew I was the fool; the
one who neglected, deceived, and lied to others. I hid in the darkness,
thinking of the resentment and animosity I had toward everyone. As my
life slowly disintegrated in front of me, the demons in my mind and soul
were getting stronger; stronger than ever before. I read somewhere that
demons could influence our thoughts—mentally and spiritually. Well,
if that is the case, they were having a field day with mine.

The thoughts that kept running through my head were unimagin-
able; the constant tormenting was getting hard to deal with. I knew that
if I continued with the way I was behaving, it would only be a matter of
time before I lost my mind. Contemplating several scenarios, other than
giving up and checking out, which ran through my mind often, I realized
that I had to do something if I was ever going to regain my sanity.

I looked everywhere for help but kept running into obstacles, which led me back to my drinking; it was easier than facing the truth. I wanted to do the right thing, but I kept falling back into that dark place in my mind, somewhere nobody should have to be. It was as if I was in a bad dream; a dream that kept haunting me; trapped in a place I hated.

I'll never forget the night I finally reached out for help. My life was over as I knew it. I was afraid, worn out, and broken. I was so depressed, I knew I had to do something, so I reached for my phone and dialed 911. The next thing I remember, I was lying on a bed in the emergency room. I had been in this situation before, but what took place this time will be with me for the rest of my life.

While there, I thought at first I was hallucinating, but a very attractive, well-dressed, brunette lady came in and sat down beside me. At first, I thought she was a staff member checking up on me, but she had no identification, no stethoscope, and wasn't carrying a clipboard. She began talking to me in a way that made me feel at ease. She told me that I was in a safe place, that I was going to be taken care of, and that everything was going to be all right. I always heard that some people experience spiritual awakenings, but it never happened to me, until now. From that point on, things started to get better in my life.

> And there appeared an angel unto him from heaven, strengthening him.
>
> Luke 22:43

During my stay in the hospital, I began to think clearly while my life slowly crept back into my body. I felt as if I were a new person, ready to take on the world. Unfortunately, I had felt like this before, so I was a little hesitant and cautious in believing everything was going to be all right. I knew my life, dreams, and destiny were in my hands, and if I screwed this up again, I would eventually end up back where I was—in that dark, dreaded place that I hated.

Part 2

After the encounter in the emergency room, which I believe was a spiritual awakening, I realized what I had to have: a life that I controlled, loved, and cherished; something that I hadn't had for quite some time. I realized that there will be times when we are going to have to listen to our conscience. My conscience was telling me to pursue what I lost years ago—my religion and beliefs. My thoughts kept telling me to put God and Jesus back in my life, become a better person, and start helping others. So my mission began.

To help others, I knew I had to help myself first. This was an up-and-down ordeal that I tried numerous times before, but I made my mind up that this time was going to be different. I was on a mission; a mission that I was destined to do. I began reading and journaling my thoughts and the things I was doing during my recovery. I began reading the Bible, support books, or anything I could get my hands on about religion, spirituality, and substance abuse. Doing this helped me tremendously understand what I needed in my recovery.

Religion

There has always been some form of religion in my life. My mother was a strong believer in God, and she instilled it in her children. I was brought up believing, but the older I got, the more I forgot. I opened the Bible several times in my life but would put it done to pursue other interests. You have heard the saying "If only I would have known…" Well, if only I would have known! How many of you have ever thought the same thing? Once I got serious about my life, my religion slowly returned. At this juncture, when all hell was breaking loose, putting religion back in my life was the best thing I could do. Talking and praying to God; reading the Bible and reaching out to those who view religion as a part of life has helped me tremendously. You should give it a try if you are struggling to understand. It doesn't hurt, I promise.

> For I the Lord thy God will hold thy right hand, saying
> unto thee, Fear not; I will help thee.
>
> Isaiah 41:13

Spirituality

Reading about spirituality has taught me that there was something out there greater than myself (this was hard to accept at first, but I got over it). Spirituality let me see a broader perspective on life. I thought about it, wrote about it, and talked about it for a long time. Self-care, self-respect, and the existence of something bigger out there has put a new meaning in my life. I learned that we should love and respect ourselves more, become one with our inner-self, and enjoy life and the things in it. Spirituality helps us pursue a sense of purpose in our lives, either through religion, nature, the universe, or through our own experiences in life.

Keeping spirituality in our lives is important. It helps in defining what the bigger picture might be, your relationships, and your overall well-being. It takes time and a lot of nurturing to develop a strong spiritual life, but it is worth it.

Substance Abuse

Educating myself about substance abuse helped me understand what I was in for with my recovery. It opened my eyes to a lot of areas I knew little about. If you want to recover from your addiction, you need to learn and understand what substance abuse is and what you are up against.

Substance abuse disorders can come from using drugs and alcohol. The more you use, the more your brain wants. They affect your brain and behavior, mentally and physically, and over time, they will slowly destroy you. In most instances, to become free of your addiction, you are going to have to reach out for help. Your family, friends, doctors, or a minister can help you decide the best course of action you should pursue.

I have many reasons to stay sober today, and if you think about it, so do you. Try to grasp what I am saying. It's your life, a life too short to continue living it the way you have been. You need to embrace it, take advantage of it, love it, and never take it for granted. What helped me the most was when I put my life in God's hands. I learned my lesson the hard way. Don't learn your lesson the same way. Reach out and ask for help before it is too late.

> Lead me in thy truth, and teach me: for thou art the God of my salvation; on thee do I wait all the day.
> Psalm 25:5

NOTES

(you will notice at the end of each chapter, I left room for notes. Please take advantage of this. If my ideas are not your cup of tea, come up with your own).

_____

_____

_____

_____

_____

_____

_____

_____

_____

_____

_____

_____

_____

_____

_____

_____

_____

_____

_____

_____

_____

_____

_____

_____

2
The Choices We Make

People have been making choices since the beginning of time.

Adam and Eve chose to eat the forbidden fruit. They were cast out of The Garden of Eden and had to live a mortal life.

Daniel, from the "Book of Daniel" chose to pray to God when everyone in the kingdom was told not to. The king sentenced him to death and threw him into the lion's den. Most of us know how that turned out.

Jesus made the ultimate choice when he chose death over running away. He chose to take the punishment for all our sins, which he knew would restore our relationship with God.

Every day, you will make choices, one way or another. If you are like me, struggling with an addiction, the choices you make can be very detrimental to your life. Your mind will tell you to make a choice to use, and you follow through. You might wake up three or four days later and wonder why you made that choice. This will happen if you are not careful.

The choices that you make will always have an impact on your life. Good or bad, they can either be your salvation or your demise. Hopefully, one day you will learn from the bad choices you have made. I will be honest with you: I made some bad choices in my life, and I had to deal with the consequences. Did I learn my lesson? Hardly! I kept on drinking and doing things I shouldn't have been doing. It took a long time for me to realize that the bad choices I was making were slowly killing me. What about you? Have you made some bad choices in your life?

I came up with a list that might help you make good choices. They worked for me.

- Choose the right path you want to be on that will help you with your recovery.
- Know the differences between good and bad choices.
- Choose places to go where you know there will not be any temptations.
- Make choices that do not have bad consequences. You will know them.
- Choose family and friends who are going to help you with your recovery. They are out there; you just need to find them.
- Remember, the choices you make can change your life forever - make sure you make the right one this time.

> I call heaven and earth to record this day against you, that I have set before you life and death, blessing and cursing: therefore choose life, that both thou and thy seed may live:
>
> Deuteronomy 30:19

It all boils down to how you plan to live your life. You are going to have to convince yourself to do what is good and stay clear of what you know is bad. It sounds easier than it actually is, but it is something that you need to do. Remember, you do not have to be a saint to make good choices in your life.

Here are two examples of actual choices made by some men I knew.

Choice One (The Wrong Choice):

He talks to an old friend he has not heard from since he stopped using. The friend invites him to come over, and he chooses to go. When he gets there, they offer him things he knows he should not be doing. He thinks about it and tells himself it will only be one time. What can that hurt, right?

He knows the consequences when he picks up the pipe full of meth. He knows what could happen, yet he chooses to do it anyway. He could choose to walk away, but he does not. Now he is back in the same situation he was in once before.

Unfortunately, he chose to indulge.

Choice Two (The Right Choice):

He sees a friend he has not seen in a while. The two of them talk and reminisce about the past. He tells his friend he has been clean and sober for quite some time and his life has not felt this good in a long time. As the two are saying goodbyes, they shake hands. While shaking hands his friend slips him a small packet of drugs. Surprised, he hands the packet back to his so-called friend and informs him that he decided to start his life over and drugs are no longer a part of it. He then tells him to have a nice life as he is walking away.

Fortunately, he chose to walk away.

So, you see, you can either choose to indulge in bad behavior or you can choose to walk away. Just remember, do not blame others for the choices you make. You made them, you have to live with them.

NOTES

3
Who Are You?

For ye are all the children of God by faith in Christ Jesus.

Galatians 3:26

Who are you? This is something you might be asking yourself right about now. I know I did. Hopefully in time, you will figure that question out. Until then, it is time for you to start planning the path you want to be on. This path is going to be hard, exceedingly difficult and challenging, yet one of the most rewarding accomplishments that you can make in your life at this time. Finding out who you are and getting back to that person you used to be will be worth more than what you are doing now with your life. There will be times when you encounter detours and roadblocks, which will try and divert you from this path. Just remember, you are the one who controls which way you go, regardless of what gets in your way. Believe me, it will take everything you have inside of you to get around them, over them, or through them. But you can do it if you put your mind in the right perspective.

Have not I commanded thee? Be strong and of a good courage; be not afraid, neither be thou dismayed: for the Lord thy God is with thee whithersoever thou goest.

Joshua 1:9

Listen, when I was that pathetically depressed and anxiety-stricken drunk I did not like, I would not accept who I was. When I looked in the mirror, which was rare, I hated who I saw, and that terrified me. Because of this, I avoided people like the plague. To be honest, I did not want to be around myself, let alone anyone else. It took me several years to figure out who I was and to honestly believe in myself; hopefully, it will not take you as long.

Figure out who you are and what you want. Start out on this path by believing that you can do whatever you put your mind to. If you let someone or something else control your thoughts, you are going to be fighting a losing battle. Get rid of the old you, the old thoughts, old habits, and those demons dancing around your head. Start believing in yourself, not the old self. I can tell you from experience that if you are not going to let go of the old you, you will never be able to grab a hold of the new you.

In time, you too will learn that it does not matter how much help you get from your family, friends, doctors, or support programs; if you do not believe in yourself, you will be destined to continue to be that person you do not like. Tell yourself that you are going to stop living in the past. Your alcohol and/or drug days are over. Tell yourself you want a new and improved life that you are in control of. You are going to have to fight if you want your life back.

> For God hath not given us the spirit of fear; but of power, and of love, and of a sound mind.
>
> 2 Timothy 1:7

Start today! Let go of the things that are controlling you and dragging you down. Do not wait! Do it now! Your addiction, whatever it may be, is slowly destroying you. It has taken control of your life, and it will not let go unless you do something about it. I fought and won this battle. You can too. Take control and stop being the weak-minded, out-of-control person you have been. Admit to yourself that you have a serious problem, and you need help. That's it! Until then, no one on the face of the Earth can help you; support groups, hospitals, and treatment centers can try, but chances are they won't work. You are going to have to search for answers that will help you with your recovery. You need to accept the fact that you are an addict.

Once you have honestly accepted that you are the problem and can tell yourself without a doubt that you need help, you will begin to recover from the sickness you have been fighting for so long. This step to recovery is demanding but can be accomplished if you have the willingness to search deep into your heart, mind, and soul.

You will find out who you are when you explore all the possibilities that are out there. Be yourself, and work on your recovery before it is too late. Your life is worth it!

I can do all things through Christ which strengtheneth me.
Philippians 4:13

NOTES

4
Reaching Out for Help

While struggling with my addiction over the last several years, I tried to recover on my own. After several attempts and failures, I realized I could not do this alone. I was going to have to find what worked best for me. I needed to find the right people to surround myself with; people who wanted to help me recover. Notice how I said, "the right people"? Believe it or not, some people do not want you to change; they like you just the way you are—high or intoxicated. You might think they are your friends, but believe me, they are not.

During your treatment or rehabilitation, you must consider who can help you. Your best bet is your family, sober friends, doctors, therapists, support groups, and theologians. Do not try to recover on your own. It is too difficult and dangerous. I tried, failed, and almost died. Don't go through what I did. Unfortunately, I know people who have died trying to do this alone. Make sure you reach out and get the help and support you need. This is a very critical time in your life. Do the right thing.

> Iron sharpeneth iron; so a man sharpeneth the countenance of his friend.
>
> Proverbs 27:17

It took me some time to find the right people to associate with, so don't think this will happen overnight. You are going to have to determine who and what is best for you during your recovery. Making the right choices now with whom you choose to be around can change your life—either in a good way or a bad way. So, choose cautiously and wisely. I cannot emphasize this enough: take your time when looking for the right people you want to share your life with. It will make a huge difference.

Do not continue to hang out with people you know are bad influences. You know who I am talking about. They are the ones who just want to get high or drunk and tell you you're doing the right thing when you know you aren't. Saying goodbye to these types of people while you are going through recovery will be the best thing you can do at this point. Then, when you are working on your recovery, you will not have to worry about them showing up. But if they do show up, they will know you mean business when you tell them to go away. Do not fall for the "it's only one time" thing. It won't be, trust me. I know I am being hard on you at this point, but I am telling you this from experience. Trust only those who want what is best for you.

> He that walketh with wise men shall be wise: but a companion of fools shall be destroyed.
> Proverbs 13:20

There are a lot of people out there who want to help. If you want your life back—a life full of hope, happiness, and success—then you are going to have to surround yourself with people who have hope, happiness, and success. Those who have been through what you have been through or at least understand what you are going through. You will need people who are going to be able to lift you mentally and spiritually, people who will be there to pick you up when you fall, and people who are going to encourage you to do better.

Don't be afraid to ask others what they think about your recovery, unless, of course, they are your former so-called friends who are still using. Stay away from them; they will tell you something completely different. Putting good people in your life will tell you the truth. You will be surprised when you hear them tell you how proud they are of you. They are the ones you want to keep close to you. They are the ones who will make your recovery possible. This is going to take time, but if you want to recover, you are going to have to do it. Remember, this is your life, no one else's. Plan it accordingly.

> Beloved, let us love one another: for love is of God; and every one that loveth is born of God, and knoweth God.
>
> 1 John 4:7

NOTES

_____

_____

_____

_____

_____

_____

_____

_____

_____

_____

_____

_____

_____

_____

_____

_____

_____

_____

_____

_____

_____

_____

_____

_____

_____

5
You Need to Stop Running

I ran for a long time. I ran from my family, my friends, my responsibilities, my spirituality, and I ran from myself. If it wasn't for me getting my life straightened out, I'd still be running. I knew if I didn't stop running and face my problems, my life was only going to get worse. You are going to have to do the same thing. Stop running from your problems, face your fears, and abandon those thoughts that are slowly destroying you. You are going to have to start thinking about everything you do in your life if you want to stay clean and sober.

Yes, it will be hard, complicated, and demanding, but it is something you are going to have to do. You are going to have to start thinking about what is going on around you, stay focused, and finally face the truth. Facing the truth was the hardest thing I had to do. How about you? Someone once told me that if I fall, get up and keep going.

> For a just man falleth seven times, and riseth up again:
> but the wicked shall fall into mischief.
>
> Proverbs 24:16

You are going to have to make changes in your life that will be hard to do at first, so don't panic or freak out. You are going to have to change your thought process. It's that simple. I was always having negative thoughts. I had to learn how to stop thinking this way. Positive thinking is the only thing that is going to save you. You are going to have to start thinking differently. You cannot debate this with yourself; if you do, you will lose and eventually give up. Never give up! This is the only way you are going to recover from your addiction.

Start focusing on yourself by clearing the cobwebs out of your head. If you don't, nothing will ever change. I'm being honest with you when I tell you that you don't want to keep heading down that terrible path of destruction you are on. Sooner or later that path will end abruptly. Then there you will be, lost and confused, not knowing which way to go. Trust me, I have been down that path.

"The Path"

I have been walking down this path for so long. I have no idea where I was going. I have not seen anyone in so long. It is getting dark outside, and I finally figure out I am all alone. I am mentally and spiritually exhausted, beaten down, and bruised. I think my life is through.

The voices I keep hearing in my head, only the demons, and I know what is being said. They continue tormenting me, constantly getting the best of me. Nowhere to go; nowhere to hide. How did I ever end up on this path I am on?

I am lost and a little confused, not knowing what to do or where to go. I think about turning around, but I remember the bridges I have burnt down. I cannot go back even if I want to.

If I could only find someone who can help me, then I might have a chance to get off this path I am on. Unfortunately for me, no one has come along. It is lonely out here, lost and alone and in despair. This was not the way I wanted things to end.

Talking to myself is getting me nowhere. My thoughts are

getting the best of me. I know I have to do something before I stumble and fall. Then I hear a voice—another demon, I thought; but no, not this time. It was the Holy Spirit within me who tells me He has been with me all along, waiting and wondering to see when I was going to reach out and ask for help.

I had no idea He was with me. So I reached out and ask for help and He came through for me. What a relief. I should have believed instead of trying to do things on my own. What a lesson I have learned! Thank you, God, for sending me help and getting me back on the path I always should have been on.

And ye shall seek me, and find me, when ye shall search for me with all your heart.

Jeremiah 29:13

Here are some quotes that helped me when I stopped running. Stop, think, learn what you read, and stay focused on the new you. The 12 things I have listed below helped me tremendously. I read them every day during my recovery. They motivated me to continue pursuing my recovery. If you are serious, they might help you as well.

Make peace with yourself.

Depart from evil, and do good; seek peace, and pursue it.

Psalm 34:14

Enjoy your life.

Rejoicing in hope; patient in tribulation; continuing instant in prayer;

Romans 12:12

Do good things.

To them who by patient continuance in well doing seek for glory and honour and immortality, eternal life:

Romans 2:7

Pray every day.

If we confess our sins, he is faithful and just to forgive us our sins, and to cleanse us from all unrighteousness.

1 John 1:9

Stop feeling sorry for yourself.

These things I have spoken unto you, that in me ye might have peace. In the world ye shall have tribulation: but be of good cheer; I have overcome the world.

John 16:33

Ask God what you can do for Him.

And it shall come to pass, if ye shall hearken diligently unto my commandments which I command you this day, to love the Lord your God, and to serve him with all your heart and with all your soul,

Deuteronomy 11:13

Become independent.

Brethren, be not children in understanding: howbeit in malice be ye children, but in understanding be men.

1 Corinthians 14:20

Read the Bible or whatever works for you.

For whatsoever things were written aforetime were written for our learning, that we through patience and comfort of the scriptures might have hope.

Romans 15:4

Enjoy the things around you.

For ye shall go out with joy, and be led forth with peace: the mountains and the hills shall break forth before you into singing, and all the trees of the field shall clap their hands.

Isaiah 55:12

Don't live in the past; what's done is done.

Remember ye not the former things, neither consider the things of old.

Isaiah 43:18

Be yourself and not someone else.

For if a man think himself to be something, when he is nothing, he deceiveth himself.

Galatians 6:3

Believe in yourself.

So that we may boldly say, The Lord is my helper, and I will not fear what man shall do unto me.

Hebrews 13:6

These quotes can help change your life and guide you in the right direction, as they did for me. If you do not like the Bible verses, change them to what works best for you. There are thousands of quotes out there that might work better for you.

Think about what you are doing right now. It doesn't get any easier the longer you wait. You are going to have to stop running. If you do not, whatever you are running from will eventually catch up with you. Then what?

Do it today because no one is guaranteed a tomorrow.

NOTES

_____

_____

_____

_____

_____

_____

_____

_____

_____

_____

_____

_____

_____

_____

_____

_____

_____

_____

_____

_____

_____

_____

_____

6
It's Your Recovery

I sometimes get asked what I think the best support group would be to help with someone's addiction, and my answer has always been YOU! You are your best support group for fighting and recovering from your addiction. Only you have that power. Sure, there will always be your family, friends, doctors, theologians, and support groups that want to help, but it is ultimately up to you to work on your recovery and program. No one else has that kind of power over you. Some may think they do, but they do not. With that said, never let anyone force, coerce, or pressure you into doing something that makes you feel uncomfortable.

The whole purpose of this book is to help those who are struggling with addiction and are uncomfortable working with support groups. I have talked with some individuals over the years that think of themselves as "loners" that do not like discussing their problems with other individuals, would rather do things quietly, and do not like getting involved with groups. I just so happen to be one of those "loners". This does not mean I do not believe in support groups. I do.

I tried a lot of groups that were offered. Unfortunately, I was just not comfortable with any of them. Support groups just were not a good fit for me. I found out that I needed something different for my life and recovery. That is why I came up with what is in this book. It works if you want it bad enough. Just remember, this does not mean that you do things alone. You still need to reach out for help as I did; it just depends on whom you reach out to. There are places that want to help you. Start looking at the options out there that are available.

You are the only one who knows what will work for you. Just remember these simple things.

- **Decide on what is going to work best for you.**
- **Find something that is going to make you feel comfortable.**
- **Do not expect this to happen overnight.**
- **Patience and perseverance helps.**
- **Work on this daily.**
- **Plan for your success.**
- **Listen to those who want to help you.**
- **Do not get angry with yourself.**
- **Only do what you know is right.**
- **Don't give up.**

Now, I know I will probably have some support groups upset with me, but it doesn't matter. I am telling you this so you can get what you need when it comes to your recovery. This book will work if you take the time and energy to follow through. It worked for me and it will work for you if you let it.

You also have to realize that this will take dedication and determination on your part. When you wake up, look in the mirror and repeat to yourself, "I CAN DO THIS." Your recovery depends on you making the right decisions in your life every day. You need to put everything that has happened behind you and move on.

> And thine ears shall hear a word behind thee, saying,
> This is the way, walk ye in it, when ye turn to the right
> hand, and when ye turn to the left.
>
> Isaiah 30:21

Note: Don't misunderstand what I am saying here: if support groups work for you, great; continue using them. If they do not, there are other alternatives out there.

What does God want?
(These are my thoughts and no one else's.)

Some theologians will tell us God wants us to be obedient and obey God's commandments. They would also probably tell us to refer to Matthew 22:37-40. Which states:

Jesus said unto him, thou shalt love the Lord thy God with all thy heart, and with all thy soul, and with all thy mind. This is the first and great commandment. And the second is like unto it, thou shalt love thy neighbour as thyself. On these two commandments hang all the law and the prophets.

I believe this is true, but I also believe that God wants us to live life to its fullest by following a path that is good. A path that will teach us and help us become a better person so one day we can do the same for others.

This path we would be on will not be an easy one to follow. It will take a conviction of faith and trust in God, ourselves, and others. It will take strength and determination to walk this path. If we do not follow the plan, the odds of staying on the path will not be in our favor.

While on this path, we cannot afford to look back. What is back there needs to stay there. The future is our destiny now. We must prepare ourselves mentally, spiritually, and emotionally today so we can prepare ourselves to move into the future tomorrow.

We need to start by changing ourselves mentally. Believe it or not, our thoughts control our destiny: good or bad. We will need to open our minds to the possibilities that are out there. We are no longer the person we once were. We need to consistently tell ourselves that we are better and stronger than we used to be.

We need to put spirituality in our lives. We need to remind ourselves we are not alone in this universe and there is something bigger than ourselves out there. We need to keep telling ourselves that the world does not revolve around us, we revolve around it. A good start is to pray, connect with nature, or start attending spiritual events, whatever that might be.

Finally, we must become emotionally fit. We need to stop letting our emotions get the best of us. We have to push out the negative thoughts that we have built up in our minds and replace them with positive ones. If we do not, those negative thoughts will eventually destroy us.

This is our lives. It is not our families, our friends, or those around us. It is up to us to make it a good one in the eyes of God.

NOTES

_____
_____
_____
_____
_____
_____
_____
_____
_____
_____
_____
_____
_____
_____
_____
_____
_____
_____
_____
_____
_____
_____
_____

7
We All Make Mistakes

He that covereth his sins shall not prosper: but whoso
confesseth and forsaketh them shall have mercy.

Proverbs 28:13

Reality check: Making mistakes in life is human nature. No one on the face
of the Earth doesn't make mistakes, including you. You need to remember
this. Now I know some people will argue this point, but here it is.

"Even normal people (define normal) make mistakes."

However, the difference between normal people and you is that
normal people learn from their mistakes and try not to repeat them,
most of the time. You, on the other hand, continue to make the same
mistakes again and again, knowing the whole time it is wrong. I know
one of my problems was telling myself that I did nothing wrong. I knew
I did, but I was telling myself I didn't. Big mistake! Do you feel like me
and think you have done nothing wrong? I know this led to a lot of my
mistakes in my life.

You will continue to make mistakes regardless. Get used to it. But
make sure you learn from them, so you do not make them again. Tell
yourself when you are thinking of making a mistake (you know what I
am talking about here: using, drinking, lying, etc.) that this is not going

to turn out well and will probably have consequences; bad consequences that might put you back in a place you don't want to be. Think before you act. Easier said than done, right?

Your thoughts can get the best of you if you let them. When your thoughts are bad, tell the demons to get out of your head and go back to hell. They will if you tell them; for how long, I have no idea. I know my damaging thoughts controlled me for the longest time, and I knew that I had to do something or I was going to continue making those stupid mistakes. I remember numerous times sitting there thinking about how I had everything: a loving family, a good job, and a great life. I never imagined in a million years the mistakes I made would cause so much grief. They caused me to be an embarrassment and a disgrace to my family. One mistake after another caused my life to fall apart. Have you ever been where I was?

Getting through all this was not easy, but with God's and other people's help, I eventually overcame those thoughts that caused me to make bad mistakes. You need to start thinking positively about everything you do, and maybe, you will see the light at the end of the tunnel that you have heard so much about. Once you crawl out of the darkness, your life will change in ways you can't even imagine.

"You Were Almost There"

You were almost there. You saw the light at the end of the tunnel you were in; the light was getting closer with every step you took. But for some reason, you stopped, turned around, and walked back into the darkness you were in.

Your reasoning cannot be explained. Everything was going your way. Then you told yourself to turn around and go back into the darkness, where you thought it would be safe. You thought the light was bad and it was there to harm you. Your fears took over and convinced you to turn around and go back in.

You were almost there, but once again you gave up. You gave up on your dreams and your beliefs while pushing your morals aside. You let it all go. Your ambitions and your faith were gone. You let them slip away. All these things you had, but you turned around and walked back in.

Then the day came when demons showed up and knocked on your door. You did the worst thing possible. You opened the door and let them in. Unless you act quickly and forcefully, those demons are there to stay, tormenting and harassing you every day. They will never go away!

You were almost there. What were you thinking? You know the pain, agony, and despair will return. For some reason, you feared the demons that were there. You know what you must do. Ask God for help to make them go away.

You are going to have to put your faith back in God if you want those demons to go away. Then you can return to the tunnel you were in, where you saw the light. You can continue on your journey and find happiness, peace, and joy at the end of the tunnel you are in.

For every one that doeth evil hateth the light, neither cometh to the light, lest his deeds should be reproved.

John 3:20

Our lives are too short and too important to spend them controlled by an addiction. Stop the madness before it stops you. Do not end up like so many others I knew: homeless, incarcerated, institutionalized, or dead. I know you are telling yourself that this will never happen to you, and I hope it doesn't, but if you don't get your life under control and stop making those mistakes, you are going to one day end up where those gentlemen I once knew did.

Anyone who is struggling with drug or alcohol addiction needs to take a long hard look at themselves and the mistakes they have made.

Think about what you are going to do and ask yourself this: Do you want to stay on the path you are on now or find the path that you need to be on? If you decided to continue with your life the way it is now, in time, it will come to an end. If you decided to find the right path, you are going to have to put every ounce of energy you have left in you to make it happen.

This is the time you need to open your mind to all the possibilities that are out there. Constantly tell yourself that you can do this. Don't continue making those mistakes that are slowly destroying you and those around you.

> A man's heart deviseth his way: but the Lord directeth his steps.
>
> Proverbs 16:9

Here are some things that helped me. They might help you.

- **Know what you are getting ready to do is wrong.**
- **Stop lying to yourself and others.**
- **Make a pact with God, not the devil.**
- **Start making amends with yourself and your family.**
- **Come up with answers instead of excuses.**
- **Know that you are not alone.**
- **Stop blaming others for your mistakes.**
- **Know the difference between right and wrong.**
- **Forgive yourself for the mistakes you have made.**

I always told myself that I was smarter than everybody else. Boy, was I wrong! I figured out quickly it was just my mind playing tricks on me. Could this be happening to you as well? Do you think you are smarter than everybody else? I know some people who think they are, but they are in jail now. Don't be fooled by the demons playing around in your mind. Continue working on those mistakes, and don't let anyone or anything stand in your way. Eliminate the fears that you have created. Remember, the devil thrives on your fears. Don't give him any ammunition.

> A good man out of the good treasure of his heart bringeth forth that which is good; and an evil man out of the evil treasure of his heart bringeth forth that which is evil: for of the abundance of the heart his mouth speaketh.
>
> Luke 6:45

NOTES

8
There Is Life After Addiction

**When I thought my life was over, I lifted myself
up and started over.**

I want to get the word out to all those suffering from substance abuse
that there is life after addiction. A life that you are in control of; a life
that is better than what you have now; and a life full of hope, happiness, and joy. This life exists and is only available for those who want
it. It will be hard, sometimes painful, full of grief, heartaches, and yes,
a lot of suffering; but it will be worth it because you are worth it. Do
not ever let anyone tell you differently. Believe me, some will try.

Being one of the many who struggled with an addiction, I hated
that dark feeling that haunted me. I fought hard to overcome my addiction to alcohol; I fought for years to no avail. Over and over, I tried,
and over and over I failed. My memories haunted me. They would take
me back to places I did not want to be. For me, my life was a living hell,
and I kept telling myself there was no hope for me. You don't need this
in your life. You can do better.

**I kept telling myself I would stop drinking tomorrow. I never
thought tomorrow might never come.**

Guilt will always be with me. I often thought that I had no chance
of ever recovering. I thought for the longest time that I would spend

the rest of my life hiding in a bottle. No worries, no pains, just a constant drunk. How many of you have been where I was? How many of you still are? You are not alone with your addiction. Millions of us are fighting and struggling like you every day.

You need to take your life back. Tell yourself that it is not too late to let your addiction go. When I was drinking, I never gave any thought to freeing myself from my addiction. I never thought about letting it go, trying to save myself, taking my life back, or starting over. Heck, I never thought about anything. I never knew my life's importance until it was almost too late. Have you ever thought this of yourself? If you have, it is time for you to act.

Someone once told me that if I got the right help, my addiction problems would go away. It took a while, but eventually, I came to my senses and started searching. The search seemed endless, but fortunately, God intervened and gave me the help I needed. What a blessing. I know you are probably thinking, *here we go…* but folks, listen: I was not a true believer. I did not attend church, I did not pray, and I did not do anything religious or spiritual. I was on a path I should not have been on. A path of destruction. My hopes, faith, ambitions, and belonging left me. Fortunately, they came back when I started believing, believing that possibilities were still out there for me. I turned to God for answers, and He came through for me. Do you have someone you can turn to? You could if you look hard enough.

If you want help and want to live a happy, sober free life, you are going to have to reach out for help; whatever that might be. I know help did not come looking for me, so I doubt it will come looking for you. There are a lot of support groups and people out there that want to help you; however, it will take time and patience on your part to find what works best for you. I suggest that you look online or go to the library and research subjects on your addiction and recovery support groups. Educate yourself, so you understand exactly what you are up against and what you need to do. Do not just take other people's word;

investigate it to be sure. Remember, this is your recovery and your life. It is up to you as to what you do with it!

After you have done a complete and thorough search, you might be surprised by what you find out about yourself. You might even realize there is more than just your addiction causing you problems. I know I did. I had some mental disorders (depression and anxiety) that I was also fighting. What a relief to know that it was not just alcohol destroying my life and well-being. Honestly, there is nothing wrong with finding this out about yourself now. At least you would know. If you feel that you are like me, seek some professional help. This does not mean you are crazy or losing your mind. Heck, I believe there is a little craziness in all of us.

Remember, no matter who you are or your age, reaching out just might help you find the answers you are seeking. There is nothing wrong with asking for help. I used to think I could do everything on my own. I was wrong.

Substance abuse and mental disorders can kill you. Stop the madness before it stops you!

> Where no counsel is, the people fall: but in the multitude of counsellors there is safety.
>
> Proverbs 11:14

I talked to a lot of people who work on their recovery every day. Here are some of the things they told me that help them with their recovery.

- **Cherish the people around you.**
- **Do not take things for granted.**
- **Know that today is a gift from God.**
- **Get involved and volunteer.**
- **Tell yourself you are wonderful.**
- **Never tell yourself you can't do it.**
- **Never think that you are a failure.**

- **Love yourself and others.**
- **Join a church or spiritual group.**
- **Share your recovery with others.**

Keep telling yourself that there is life after addiction. Believe me, this will change your life forever. You will begin to start liking yourself; you will be a better member of your family, and people will want to start spending time with you again. Your past life is behind you, and your new life has just begun. Live your life to its fullest and enjoy it.

> Therefore if any man be in Christ, he is a new creature: old things are passed away; behold, all things are become new.
>
> 2 Corinthians 5:17

NOTES

_____

_____

_____

_____

_____

_____

_____

_____

_____

_____

_____

_____

_____

_____

_____

_____

_____

_____

_____

_____

_____

_____

_____

9
A Recovery That Works

And the Lord shall guide thee continually, and satisfy thy soul in drought, and make fat thy bones: and thou shalt be like a watered garden, and like a spring of water, whose waters fail not.

Isaiah 58:11

When I was fighting my addiction, which was most of the time, I tried everything that was offered. I spent numerous days in treatment centers, psychiatric wards, and rehabilitation centers. Doctors and counselors tried everything except a lobotomy. Fortunately for me, in time, I was able to finally find what I needed. Something that worked for me.

There are several programs out there that will work; you are just going to have to decide what is best for you. It will take some homework on your part to find one, but it will be worth it. Ask around or go online. If you are having problems with your income, look for non-profit organizations that offer programs that are free or with little expense.

I chose a Christian-based rehabilitation program, a program that works closely with the teachings of Jesus Christ and the Bible. It was a six-month program that offered counseling services, recovery meetings, meals, and a place to stay. I knew I needed a long-term program because short-term programs were not working for me. This was right up my alley. They also helped me get closer to God; something that I needed desperately. This program worked for me. If you think this is something that would work for you, search 6-month rehabilitation programs online, at your church, or at the library.

> **"If you want a change in your life, you are going to have to start by changing yourself first."**

If you have exhausted every short-term recovery program, such as a treatment center, it might be time to do some research on a long-term recovery program. Sometimes it takes some of us longer to recover from our addiction. This doesn't mean anything is wrong with you; it just means you need more time. I did, and I am living a life without my addiction. It all depends on how bad you want this.

> **"He who has power over the mind controls the heart and soul. Build a spiritual fortress around yourself so you will be protected from those wanting to control you."**

If you are ready, here are some things that will help you prepare yourself.

- **Have a plan for what you are going to do.** I cannot emphasize this enough. This is something that usually cannot be done overnight. It will take a lot of research on your part to figure out what is going to be best for you.
- **Do this for you.** If you have not made up your mind to quit, you won't. Believe me, I tried quitting for others, and it did not work.
- **If you have someone you can talk to, other than your dealer, do so.** They might be able to help you decide what path you should pursue.

- **When you are in a program, take it seriously.** Your life depends on it. Listen and get involved with whatever program you are in. Get something out of it.
- **When you complete the program, take what you learned with you.** DO NOT leave it at the door on your way out. I have seen this happen so many times, which resulted in relapses.
- **Believe in yourself!** You have the power to do this. It wouldn't hurt to have someone else with you, such as God.

Wherefore, my beloved brethren, let every man be swift to hear, slow to speak, slow to wrath:

James 1:19

NOTES

_____

_____

_____

_____

_____

_____

_____

_____

_____

_____

_____

_____

_____

_____

_____

_____

_____

_____

_____

_____

_____

_____

_____

_____

_____

_____

_____

_____

10
Stay the Course

> I press toward the mark for the prize of the high calling
> of God in Christ Jesus.
>
> Philippians 3:14

You have worked hard to get off the addiction you have been struggling with. Your recovery was grueling and tedious. You thought the rehabilitation was going to kill you. It took some time, but you finally did it. Those terrible days are behind you, and it is time to move on, relax, and enjoy life.

Stop!

You may think you have your addiction under control; however, your recovery has just begun. It is far from being over. I know this is hard to accept, but unfortunately, this is the truth for a lot of us. I know if I don't continue doing what I am doing with my recovery every day, I will end up right back in that place I hated. When you first get out of any recovery program (treatment or rehabilitation), the worst thing you can do is to tell yourself that you are okay. You are not okay. Your recovery has just begun. If you are not careful, you might put yourself right back in that place you just left. I have seen this happen a lot. You could relapse and start that vicious cycle over.

Let thine eyes look right on, and let thine eyelids look straight before thee.

Proverbs 4:25

Stay the course!

Here is a quick story about me.

When I had a couple of months of sobriety, I started telling myself I was all right. I stopped taking my medication, stopped talking to God, stopped talking to others in recovery, and the worst thing I did was tell myself that a couple of drinks would be okay. This did not go well for me. I relapsed and had to start all over again with treatment, rehabilitation, and recovery.

How about you? Have you ever thought you were all right and could go back to the way things used to be? If you have, I hope you didn't. If you haven't thought about this, prepare yourself, because one day you will. Don't put yourself back in a position that you know will cause problems for you and others. Plan for the unexpected, and stay the course.

While staying at a rehabilitation center, I saw a lot of men come into the six-month program. They worked on their recovery, completed the program, and then left. Within one to two months, if not sooner, they relapsed. Why do you think this happened? Well, I will tell you. They didn't take what they learned with them. They left it at the door because they thought everything was all right. It wasn't. They are now right back where they were before they came to the program.

Wherever you are, plan your exit. Know what you are going to do and how you are going to do it. Never forget what you learned. Programs help you and give you advice; don't ever forget this. If you do, things might not turn out the way you want them to.

Here is a list of things I put together for myself. I told myself these every day, and I often refer back to them. I was prepared just in case the demons paid me a visit.

- Take what you learned with you.
- Don't think for a second, you are cured.
- Work on your recovery every day.
- Stay focused on the positive aspects of your life.
- Avoid temptations and things that might trigger you.
- Avoid distractions that might arise.
- If you put spirituality in your life, keep it there.
- Do not think about getting back with your using friends.
- Stay close to those who helped you. Have their names and numbers.
- No matter how hard it gets, keep pushing yourself.

If this list doesn't work for you, make up your own. You must have a plan of action. If you do not, your chance of continuing your recovery is slim—regardless of what you think. There are things around every corner in life that will tempt you. Have a plan of attack for when you run into them. Don't let your mind wander, if you do, you could relapse.

> Watch ye, stand fast in the faith, quit you like men, be strong.
>
> 1 Corinthians 16:13

Stay the course!

NOTES

_____
_____
_____
_____
_____
_____
_____
_____
_____
_____
_____
_____
_____
_____
_____
_____
_____
_____
_____
_____
_____
_____
_____
_____
_____
_____
_____
_____

11
Trust Yourself First

Trust in the Lord with all thine heart; and lean not unto thine own understanding.

Proverb 3:5

Something I never gave much thought to was when it came to trusting myself. For the longest time, I thought everything was fine. I didn't think about trust being a factor in my life, especially when it came to trusting myself. It wasn't until I started making some poor decisions in my life that I realized I needed to examine my trustworthiness before I could move on to bigger and better things. So, one of my first challenges was to figure out how I was going to start trusting myself.

**Do you trust yourself? You might say you do,
but do you?**

After racking my brain on this, which wasn't easy, I found ways that worked for me. There are a couple of things I did that you could try. But you are going to have to open up your mind and believe if you want them to work.

One thing that worked, and still does, was repeating affirmations to myself that I came up with. I started small and easy, with two to three affirmations. After these started to sink in, I moved on to longer and more difficult ones. These affirmations gave me emotional strength, which helped me when I needed it the most. They might even help you. Come up with your own or just use mine. They are not hard but have to be said every day if you want them to work.

Here were my first ones:

"I am ready for this."

"I can do it."

"I will make this happen today."

Pretty simple, right? What works best is when you repeat them to yourself in front of a mirror. It will help you build self-esteem and confidence. Something I needed badly.

> What time I am afraid, I will trust in thee.
>
> Psalm 56:3

Once these are working for you, move on to new, more difficult ones. Affirmations will work if you give them a chance. Patience helps.

Don't give up or tell yourself they are not working. You are going to have to commit yourself to these in order for them to work. Don't make it complicated; be truthful, and work on them every day. If you cannot think of any affirmations, just look "affirmations" up on the internet. There are hundreds of them out there.

Another thing that helped me with my trust was things I should have been telling myself all along.

- **Block out negative thoughts.**
- **Stop thinking about the past.**
- **Confide in yourself.**

- **Love yourself for who you are.**
- **Be strong and courageous.**
- **Show others that you are serious about your recovery.**
- **Live a happy life.**
- **Put God in your life.**
- **Work on your self-esteem.**
- **Remember that you can be your worst enemy.**

The battle you are fighting right now is in your head. It will probably be one of the hardest battles you have at this point in your life. Being able to conquer this battle will allow you to conquer more things throughout your life. Trust me!

> O give thanks unto the Lord; for he is good: because his mercy endureth for ever.
>
> Psalm 118:1

NOTES

12
We Are Not Alone

> Fear thou not; for I am with thee: be not dismayed; for I am thy God: I will strengthen thee; yea, I will help thee; yea, I will uphold thee with the right hand of my righteousness.
>
> Isaiah 41:10

When I was overwhelmed and had no direction in my life, I turned to God and asked Him for help. I knew He was the only one who would be able to take away all the pain, heartaches, and worries I was suffering from. I knew that my salvation and my life were better off under His care. I knew He would guide me and lead me out of the darkness that I was in for so long, and I truly believed, for the first time in my life, that there was a God and He wanted to help me overcome the troubles I was enduring.

> Teaching them to observe all things whatsoever I have commanded you: and, lo, I am with you always, even unto the end of the world. Amen.
>
> Matthew 28:20

I know you are going through a lot right now, and it seems at times that things are not getting any better with your life. I understand; I have been where you are. Putting spirituality back into your life might be what you need at this time. There is nothing wrong with believing in a power that is greater than you. I finally conceded to the care of God. He helped me when I needed it the most. Who can you put in your life?

What you are struggling with will only get worse, I assure you. So prepare yourself now and start telling yourself that you are going to recover from this addiction you have. Putting God in your life would be a good start, believe me. When I asked for help, God answered me through my family, the Holy Spirit, and yes, even through the internet. Crazy right? Every time something happened, unexpectedly in my life, I credited God. I knew He was making these things happen.

If you can come to terms with a power greater than yourself. You are on your way. It might take some time to figure out just what you need. Talk to others that have found spirituality. It can help you beyond your imagination. God has been with us since the beginning of time. I think He knows what we need.

Starting over is not going to be easy. You will figure out quickly that the path you are on will be a slippery one. Having someone with you helps. You will face challenges, obstacles, and detours along the way. Do not panic. You are not alone. There will be family members, friends, angels, and yes, even demons, waiting and watching you. You will have to be careful, or you might slip back into the darkness you are fighting so hard to get out of. You might even find yourself praying every day, asking God for guidance. There is nothing wrong with doing this. It saved me!

There will be times you want to give up and return to your old ways. You will catch yourself at times trying to persuade yourself that you were better off the way you were. You might even want to hide and isolate yourself from the world around you. At times, voices may be telling you that you are worthless; that you are a loser; or criticize and harass you. Other times they may be making fun of you, telling you you're not good enough and that your life is meaningless. Dismiss these voices and thoughts. They are demons trying to control your mind. You will need to constantly remind yourself that it is all in your head; that the demons are trying to do everything they can to get you back to where you used to be. You need to be strong, now more than ever; but most of all, you need to have God or whomever your higher power is there for guidance.

> Be strong and of a good courage, fear not, nor be afraid of them: for the LORD thy God, he it is that doth go with thee; he will not fail thee, nor forsake thee.
>
> Deuteronomy 31:6

You have a long path ahead of you, and your life is going to have its ups and downs; complications, chaos; and confusion. That's life. All you can do is head in the direction you have chosen and accept life on life's terms; do what you are doing and believe—believe in yourself, your family, God, and the Spirits that surround you.

I have finally taken control of my life. Powerful and free; my dreams and visions are now within reach. When they become a reality, I will take a hold of them and never let them go. Long story short, I closed the door on God, but God kept on knocking and wouldn't go away. I now pray and thank God every day. Who do you want in your life?

If you believe, truly believe, God can help and guide you the way he has helped and guided me. He is there for you, waiting for you to reach out. However, if you do not ask, you may never know.

We are never alone!

Note: If you do not have God as your higher power, that is all right. However, you need to have someone in your life that you truly believe in that will help you with your recovery.

NOTES

13
You Have to Convince Yourself

As soon as Jesus heard the word that was spoken, he saith unto the ruler of the synagogue, Be not afraid, only believe.

Mark 5:36

It all begins with you. You need to convince yourself that you want to change. No one else can do this for you; it is solely up to you. Do not be afraid to start over. Start out by getting familiar with what I have written below. It helped me!

- **Know that God is real.**
- **Be careful whom you trust.**
- **Get spiritually fit.**
- **Lead people; don't follow them.**
- **Challenge yourself every day.**
- **Find good friends who want what you want.**
- **Learn how to say NO.**
- **Don't let others pressure you.**
- **Don't let people distract you.**
- **Do not take things for granted.**

We often tell ourselves "only if." Only if what? Only if I could do it all over again? Do you think you would? If you think you would, why not do it now? You are going to have to start telling yourself that you want to change your life. You are going to have to tell yourself that you want sobriety, happiness, and love in your life. No one else can tell you this. It is your life and your decision. Convince yourself you can do this!

> Be sober, be vigilant; because your adversary the devil, as a roaring lion, walketh about, seeking whom he may devour:
>
> 1 Peter 5:8

If you want to change, one of the things you need to do is believe! Believe in yourself, in others, and believe spiritually. There are so many things you are missing out on. Stop and think! Think about what you are doing to yourself and others. It is never too late to get your life back.

> Jesus said unto him, If thou canst believe, all things are possible to him that believeth.
>
> Mark 9:23

Imagine what it would be like waking up every morning, knowing that your life was back on track; no more hangovers or coming down from the drugs you were on the night before. What if you truly believed in yourself? Don't you think the possibilities would be endless? This all can happen if you just give in by letting go of the demons that are controlling you. Yes, believe it or not, they are there, in your mind, trying to destroy you.

Once you let go and start believing in yourself, you will start thinking, your mind will open, and you will start working on your life's ambitions, your dreams, and your destiny. Convince yourself that all this is possible.

"If you don't do something with your dreams, dreams are all they will ever be. Work on making your dreams come true."

When you realize that the impossible is now possible, you will start reaching out to those who want to help you, like your family, friends, support groups, and church. Keep telling yourself you can. Look for those who will be there for you; the ones who want what you want; the ones who will never give up on you; and the ones who share your beliefs – spiritually and emotionally.

"If you tell yourself, you can't, you won't. If you tell yourself, you can, you eventually will!"

NOTES

_____

_____

_____

_____

_____

_____

_____

_____

_____

_____

_____

_____

_____

_____

_____

_____

_____

_____

_____

_____

_____

_____

_____

_____

_____

_____

_____

_____

14
Enemies Within

> Keep thy heart with all diligence; for out of it are the
> issues of life.
>
> Proverbs 4:23

Enemies within, demons in your head that make you do things that you will regret. We all have them, hiding in our minds, waiting for the perfect opportunity to show themselves. Most normal (define normal) people can control them; but people who have some form of substance abuse or disorder can't or won't.

These demons lurk around our subconscious just waiting for the right time to pounce on us. For some of us, these demons will do everything they can to make our life a living hell. They will try and control our actions, thoughts, feelings, and our well-being. They have no remorse whatsoever. If we continue to allow them to influence our lives, they will eventually destroy us. They will keep tempting us to do what we know we should not be doing.

However, there are ways to deal with these unruly demons.

> Submit yourselves therefore to God. Resist the devil,
> and he will flee from you.
>
> James 4:7

One path you can take is to seek professional help from psychiatrists, counselors, and therapists. They have been trained in the fields of substance abuse, addictions, and disorders. They can help you figure out what you might need to get those demons out of your head. I was fortunate. I found a great psychiatrist who helped me a lot.

Another path, which also worked for me, is to put spirituality in your life by opening your mind and tapping into all the possibilities; realizing that there is something greater than yourself out there. You need to invest time in your spirituality, regardless of what it might be. Search for answers that you have been seeking so you can become one with yourself.

You are going to have to build and secure a strong mental foundation in your mind if you want this to work. This will not be easy, but with positive thinking, self-motivation, strong morals, self-esteem, spirituality, trustworthiness, and finally, trust in yourself and whomever you believe in, it will be possible to make a better life for yourself.

You are going to have to break away from these demons and believe in yourself if you are ever going to get rid of the enemies within you. There is a better life out there, folks, but it is going to take a clean, sober, and fearless mind to make it happen.

> Put on the whole armour of God, that ye may be able
> to stand against the wiles of the devil.
>
> Ephesians 6:11

NOTES

15
Avoid Temptations at All Costs

And lead us not into temptation, but deliver us from evil: For thine is the kingdom, and the power, and the glory, for ever. Amen.

Matthew 6:13

So, you think you have it all figured out? You know exactly what you want out of life and how you are going to get it. I knew some gentlemen much like you who thought they had it all figured out, but temptation got the best of them. One thought, one drink at a bar would be all right; that one drink led to another. Those drinks eventually killed him. Another one thought it would just be one time with friends. One hit off that pipe; he ended up taking his life. Then, I knew one who thought he could do it all by himself. His body told him differently. He died from a heart attack. The last one I'll talk about thought he was smarter than everyone else; no way would he get caught. He's now serving a life sentence behind bars. So tell me, do you think you really have it all figured out?

"It will never happen to me" thoughts can destroy you if you are not careful. You are going to have to fight this with all the power you have. Believe me, temptations are all around you. You are going to have to avoid them at all costs. Don't be a statistic like the ones I knew. Be a survivor!

Temptations come in many disguises—families, friends, events, and from within your mind. A lot of people give in to these temptations, while others who want to be free from their addiction will fight them. I strongly suggest that you fight, or you might end up like the ones I just mentioned. Knowing how to avoid them will be the key to your success and survival.

> But every man is tempted, when he is drawn away of his own lust, and enticed.
>
> James 1:14

How to avoid temptation:

- **Stay away from people and places you know will tempt you.**
- **Know what tempts you.**
- **Look the other way.**
- **Have an escape plan.**
- **Run away—don't walk.**
- **Visualize the consequences.**
- **Call someone you trust and believe in.**
- **Discipline yourself.**
- **Keep telling yourself you can do this.**
- **Believe in yourself.**

When temptation strikes:

- **Go for a walk.**
- **Read a book.**
- **Take a cold shower.**
- **Go to the library or a meeting.**
- **Reward yourself for not giving in.**

- **Tell your demons to go back to hell.**
- **Relax and take deep breaths.**
- **Trust yourself to do the right thing.**
- **Talk to someone who can help you.**
- **Remember what happens when you give in.**

These examples worked for me. Prepare yourself and be ready. Think positively about yourself regardless of the circumstance. Remember, the consequences will be far worse for you if you just give in to the temptations.

"No – one of the easiest words to say in the English dictionary, yet one of the hardest words to do!"

NOTES

16
Mental Disorders Can Kill You

There was a time when I thought that it was only my addiction to alcohol that was slowly killing me. I had no idea that I was dealing with some mental disorders. It took several doctors and therapists to figure out that there was more than just my addiction hurting me. They concluded that alcohol and some disorders were controlling my life. How many of you might be dealing with a disorder you are not aware of? Do you ever think to yourself that there might be something else wrong with you? I have worked with a lot of people who have told me they might need help with more than their addiction. If you feel like we did, get help now. Don't dismiss these concerns.

There are psychiatrists, therapists, and counselors who can help you. Talk to your primary care doctor and ask them to recommend someone for you. When you see someone, make sure you tell them everything that is going on in your life. Don't lie or make things up. Tell them the truth about yourself. If you don't, they may make the wrong diagnosis. If they put you on medication, take it. It works, believe me.

Disorders can control your thoughts and your way of life. Don't be ashamed to ask for help. You are not alone when it comes to mental disorders. You might be surprised how many people have asked for help with this problem. Disorders will attack anyone at any time. They show no remorse, and they do not discriminate. Disorders can kill you just like your addiction. So stop listening to those little voices in your head.

Getting help just might get rid of them. I know those voices got the best of me, and if I would not have reached out for help, they would still be there, tormenting me. Are they tormenting you, too?

Substance abuse and disorders are common among a lot of us. We turn to our drug of choice to relieve our grief and/or bad thoughts from the past, or just trying to escape. Unfortunately, there are a lot of people out there who have no idea that the combination can be deadly. Here are a few I once knew that fall under what I have been talking about.

> I have fought a good fight, I have finished my course, I
> have kept the faith:
>
> 2 Timothy 4:7

He was doing everything right: completed a six-month rehabilitation program, gained employment, and got his own place. Everything was looking up for him. Then depression came back into his life. Not being able to handle the stress, the pressure, and not wanting to seek help, he resorted back to his old habit, heroin. Soon after that, he took his life. He was 43.

Everything was going fine. Life, friends, and work were working out well for him. He had everything that he needed. Then one day, someone from his past offered him some drugs. He hesitated but took them anyway. He overdosed on the mixture he was given. While hospitalized, he sank back into the dark place he fought so hard to get out of. He died in an assisted living home shortly after his overdose. He was 32.

He was a great guy. He cared about others in ways no one else did. He was there when you needed him, always lending a hand. Unfortunately, he just couldn't give up his addiction to alcohol. He tried several times to no avail. The last time he tried to stop, he tried doing it alone. His body had had enough. His heart quit on him. He was 46.

He began to get comfortable with his recovery. His medication was doing its job. He had done enough and thought he was cured of his addiction. He decided that it would be all right to have one drink. Several days later, intoxicated, he took a bad fall. He never recovered and passed away a few days later. He was 59.

Depressed and lonely, he distanced himself from his family through anger and grief. He started to get down on himself and started drinking. Doctors and family members told him he should not be drinking due to his health. He didn't listen. He slipped into a coma and never woke up. He was 56.

> All go unto one place; all are of the dust, and all turn to dust again.
>
> Ecclesiastes 3:20

These are just a few of the good men I had the pleasure of knowing. The hurt and sorrow will one day fade away, but I know they will always be in my heart. I will always remember the way they used to be.

Do not let something you cannot see, harm you more than it already has. Explore the possibilities and seek help. Stop letting things control your life. You are better than this.

NOTES

17
It Could Happen to You

I had a plan just in case something happened to me during my addiction days. My family knew what I wanted to be done with my remains if I were to die. I think it would be a good idea if you had a plan just in case. So if something were to happen to you, like dying, they would know what you would like done with your remains. That is if they care or even still talking to you. Just make sure you let them know that since you did not care about yourself while you were alive, it doesn't really matter what they do with you now that you are dead.

I know, lunacy, right? But the truth is, if you continue with your addiction, something is bound to happen sooner or later. These are my thoughts, not yours, so make the right move now before it is too late. That's just the way it is. I have seen it happen to those who thought nothing would ever happen to them; next thing you know, they are gone. Unlike me, they didn't have a plan. Here are some options that I came up with if I were to die. You might want to have a plan of your own, just in case.

Option One:
If you want to be buried, think about this first. An average funeral can cost about $7,000. Of course, it depends on what your family decides, such as a coffin, vault, plot, flowers, etc. You could just tell them to

throw you in a wooden box, it would be cheaper. Besides, you will not care; you are dead.

Option Two:

Cremation is my choice. It is not that expensive, and it is quick. They throw you in a box if they have one, and then they throw you in their oven. Turn up the heat, and there you are, ashes. Just make sure you tell your family what to do with your ashes. My advice would be to tell them to just flush them down the toilet, pretty much what you did with your life while you were alive.

Option Three:

If you are homeless when you die, you do not have to worry about anything. When someone finds your body, wherever it might be—under a bridge, in an alley, or in a ditch, they will take you to the city morgue for processing. Once there, they will not find any identification on you because someone robbed your body while it was lying wherever, so they tag you as John Doe, Jane Doe, or whatever Doe you might be. After 30 days, if your body goes unclaimed, they will give your body to a funeral home. That is if one will take you. They will then cremate your body and put your ashes somewhere. They are supposed to bury them in a local cemetery, but who knows? Regardless of what they do with the ashes, you are still just dust in the wind. But again, you will not care; you are dead.

You do understand what I am trying to say here, right? If you continue with your addiction, it just might lead to your demise. It is just a matter of time. Stop your addiction while you can. It is never too late to take back your life.

NOTES

_____

_____

_____

_____

_____

_____

_____

_____

_____

_____

_____

_____

_____

_____

_____

_____

_____

_____

_____

_____

_____

_____

_____

_____

18
It's Time to Grow Up

Over the last several years, I have spent a lot of my time working with men struggling with addictions. One thing that I found interesting is how many men rely on their parents or family for support. Not moral support, but support—money, living arrangements, or whatever. It did not matter what their ages were—twenties, thirties, and even into their fifties. Thinking about this, I then remembered I had a brother who did this to my mom and family. Everything he could get from us, he took. Do you know someone like this?

My question is: When are you going to start living without your parents' or your family's help? When are you going to grow up?

> When I was a child, I spake as a child, I understood as
> a child, I thought as a child: but when I became a man,
> I put away childish things.
>
> 1 Corinthians 13:11

Folks, don't you think it is time to stop relying on your families so they can enjoy their own lives? Don't you think they worry enough about you? They do not need you asking them for something every time they turn around. You are all adults, so act like it. One day, they will be gone. Then what? It is time for you to grow up and start accepting responsibility for your life. It is time for you to become independent and accountable for your own actions. Live your life, and let your parents and family live theirs.

They love you and apparently will do anything for you, but you are slowly pulling them down into that hole you are in. Your addiction is affecting them every day you keep using. Believe it or not, they are hurting inside. Can you imagine what is going through their minds? Do you even care, or is it all about you? Do you blame them for your problems? Have you ever thought that you are the problem? Probably not! Unfortunately for you, it is your problem and not someone else's.

The reason I am being so hard with you on this is to get you to realize that one day they may just "go away." Then what? You need to start working on your addiction and troubles on your own and with trained professionals or groups designed to help.

Your family can be there for moral support, but that should be all.

Good luck!

NOTES

19
For the Family

I put this section here for families just in case they were reading my book.

> Seek the LORD and his strength, seek his face continually.
> 1 Chronicles 16:11

There you are, watching a loved one suffering from the pain of an addiction, an addiction that is slowly killing them. You never thought it would come to this. You never thought it could happen to someone you know and love, but it did. Whatever the addiction—drugs or alcohol—it has slowly taken over their lives and yours. They are in a dark place in their lives, and the walls are slowly collapsing in on them. Their only hope is to reach out to the only support they have, which could be you.

During my time struggling with my addiction, I often turned to my family for help. They were there in the beginning, but after letting them down so many times, they had to finally cut me off. You too can be there for your loved ones in the beginning; however, it is up to you as to how long you stay there. You will figure this out in time; I know my family did. Just be careful. Their addiction can take a toll on you as it has them, mentally, which will cause you problems you don't need. So be prepared!

And we know that all things work together for good to them that love God, to them who are the called according to his purpose.

Romans 8:28

Your first thought is to do whatever it takes to help, but you are at a loss; you are asking yourself; how could this have happened? Believe it or not, this happens more than people think. It doesn't matter who you are or where you come from. Substance abuse, such as drugs and alcohol, doesn't care. It will grab anyone regardless of their stature. Their bodies and minds will become dependent on it, and eventually, they will become dependent on you if they aren't already. This is where you are going to have to be ready.

When your loved one begins reaching out, it could come in several ways. They might want to get treatment, which is great; or they might just want what you are willing to give them: money, a place to stay, food, or sympathy. I know this because I have been on both sides as an addict and a loved one trying to help. They want whatever you have that will keep them going. Money plays a big part in this. Go figure. If you have it, they will want it.

One thing to watch out for is to never underestimate your loved ones who are struggling with an addiction; they are smarter than you think. They might lie, steal, beg, or deceive you out of whatever you have; they might tell you what you want to hear and then do just the opposite; and at times, they might tell you they love you, and other times, they might tell you they despise you. With that said, don't let your guard down or turn your back on them. Prepare for the worse possible scenarios and try not to take it too personally. Some of the time, they have no idea what they are doing or saying.

Casting all your care upon him; for he careth for you.

1 Peter 5:7

Getting involved with the one struggling will be challenging for you. Try and get them to talk to you about their problems, but don't force or demand anything. They might rebel and turn against you. Remember, you are just trying to get them to talk to you; they are going to have to be the ones that decide they need help. If they don't think they have a problem or need help, there is very little you will be able to do for them. They are going to have to want this for themselves.

Here are a few ideas that might help you:

- **Start by getting help for yourself. Don't try to do this alone. Seek help from a professional (counselors, therapists, etc.), your church, or support groups (Al-Anon/Alateen, etc.).**
- **Be patient with them throughout their recovery. Take it one step at a time.**
- **Make sure the one you're helping wants help.**
- **Learn to say "NO." This is harder than you might think, trust me!**
- **Stand your ground. Do not let them walk all over you. They will try to.**
- **Be supportive, but don't give in. They need you now more than ever.**
- **Don't think the worst about them. Substance abuse can happen to anyone.**
- **Make sure they know you care, and you love them.**
- **Learn about substance abuse and get involved with support groups.**
- **Never give up on them. Keep them in your prayers.**

You are about to take part in something that just might be the hardest thing you have ever done with a family member or friend. You are going to have to be patient with them. If everything works out for you and your loved one, continue doing what you are doing.

Saving someone from an addiction isn't easy; however, if you are successful, you might have just saved their life. So be careful, respectful to a point, and prepared. You might have to do things that you don't want to do. There may come a time when you have to walk away and distance yourself from them until they get better. As I stated earlier, this isn't going to be easy.

My life was just like your loved ones'. I didn't care about anyone. All I cared about was drinking and being alone. There were a lot of times I reached out to my family for help. They would come to my aid and then I would go and do something stupid again.

Finally, they had had enough. My wife left me, and my daughter was disgusted with me. They were done dealing with my addiction, not me. They loved me, but they were through with what I was doing to myself. If my family did not walk away when they did, I have no doubt that I would have never recovered.

"When we help those that have lost their way, we help save a Soul. Reach out and help someone today."

NOTES

_____
_____
_____
_____
_____
_____
_____
_____
_____
_____
_____
_____
_____
_____
_____
_____
_____
_____
_____
_____
_____
_____
_____
_____

20
It Takes Time

I've seen a lot of men come through the rehabilitation program. Some complete the program while others can't even make it a week. Their addiction calls to them, and they take off. While running away, they forget about the consequences that await them. The only thing on their mind is to get high or drunk as quickly as they can. When they come down from whatever high they are on, they find some way to find more, and off to the races they go. Sobriety is not in their vocabulary.

Some of the ones who do complete the program wait at least two to four weeks before sliding back into their addiction. They forget what they learned and give up on themselves. This is so sad. Society tells us at an early age to stay away from illicit drugs, while alcohol should be used in moderation if you are going to drink , which is good advice for most people; however, for some reason, some of us failed to take heed of that advice. We thought our way was better. Unfortunately, our way has killed, crippled, or mentally disabled a lot of us over time. You would think we would have learned our lesson, but no; we keep digging that hole until it reaches at least six feet

> So teach us to number our days, that we may apply our hearts unto wisdom.
>
> Psalm 90:12

There are answers out there if you look hard enough for them. Like how many attempts does it take to quit your addiction? I actually have no idea. I have heard that it can take one or up into the teens. It all depends on the individual and the severity of the addiction. It took me seven times. Six were disastrous. The seventh time, I started believing in myself and started doing things that worked for me. I put lists together and followed them daily. You need to do the same. Believe me, they work! If you don't like mine, you need to come up with some of your own that will work for you.

- **Ask the spirit within you for help.**
- **Start believing in yourself.**
- **Tell yourself "You can do this."**
- **Start a journal.**
- **Get professional help.**
- **Put people in your life that you trust.**
- **Realize you are the problem.**
- **Know that you can be your worst enemy.**
- **Put the past behind you.**
- **Be dedicated and willing during your recovery.**

Think before you do something crazy. Once you fall off the path to recovery, you might be right back where you were before. Spend time every day working on your recovery. Do the right thing by believing it will work for you. Do not give up or give in. Your life depends on it.

> See then that ye walk circumspectly, not as fools, but as wise, redeeming the time, because the days are evil. Wherefore be ye not unwise, but understanding what the will of the Lord is.
>
> Ephesians 5:15-17

NOTES

_____

_____

_____

_____

_____

_____

_____

_____

_____

_____

_____

_____

_____

_____

_____

_____

_____

_____

_____

_____

_____

_____

_____

21
You're Never a Nobody

I was at a spiritual retreat, and a good friend of mine looked at me and said, "You know, I am a nobody." Maybe it was because we were watching how other people were acting. I'm not sure. But I do remember looking at him and saying, "You're never a nobody." You may think you are, and some people may think you are, but you're not. In the eyes of God and those who love you, you will never be a nobody. Avoid people who think of you as "a nobody" at all costs.

> Since thou wast precious in my sight, thou hast been honourable, and I have loved thee: therefore will I give men for thee, and people for thy life.
>
> Isaiah 43:4

Other people to avoid are the ones who think they are better than everyone else. I see them a lot. Sure, they may have more money, more fame, and more material things, but I assure you, they are not better than you. In fact, most of them are arrogant, conceited, and ridiculously in love with themselves. Who wants that? Eleanor Roosevelt once said, "No one can make you feel inferior without your consent." Please remember what she said.

> But he giveth more grace. Wherefore he saith, God resisteth the proud, but giveth grace unto the humble.
>
> James 4:6

I have dealt with people like this all my life. I was mostly on the receiving end. Go figure. Today, I look the other way because I know I have God and people in my life who love me for who I am. If you know or have people in your life who act like the ones I have mentioned, let them go. You do not need them in your life. If you let them stay, they could be detrimental to your recovery. You don't need people telling you that you are "no good" or that "you will never amount to anything." I am sure you have told yourself that enough! Don't let others remind you.

> Let nothing be done through strife or vainglory; but in lowliness of mind let each esteem other better than themselves.
>
> Philippians 2:3

Make sure you stay around people who are going to show you respect and who will treat you with kindness. You need this in your life right now. Heck, we all need this in our lives right now! It also wouldn't hurt to follow some examples I have listed below.

- **Avoid people who think they are better than you.**
- **Stay away from people who gossip. When you are not around them, they may be gossiping about you.**
- **Tell yourself that you are important.**
- **Do not judge others.**
- **Smile, a lot!**
- **Tell yourself that the people around you have problems as well.**
- **Remind yourself that no one is perfect, including you.**
- **Do good things for others.**
- **Obey God's commandments.**
- **Make every day count.**

You can make your life more enjoyable by thinking of yourself as a normal (define normal) person living a normal life. I remember what someone told me once. "What someone thinks of me is none of my business and what I think of them is none of theirs."

**"Being rich and famous might get you to Heaven,
but it will take wisdom and faith to get you in."**

NOTES

22
Never Give Up

I never imagined that I would spend several years of my life the way I did. At one time, I had everything going for me, but unfortunately, I let my addiction take over, and like most addictions, it had a hold on me that wouldn't let go. I fought and lost the battle of recovery so many times. How many times have you been in my situation; lost and helpless, and when you needed help, there was no one around? How many times have you ever thought that your life had no direction or meaning, and you didn't know what to do or which way to go? It happens, folks; but there is a way out.

First, never give up on yourself. If you do, you might as well crawl back into the darkness you were in. It is up to you to stay out of that place you do not like. It can destroy you. Secondly, believe in others who want to help you, but beware of those who don't. Pretty simple, right? I know, you are thinking I'm nuts, but this helped me when I finally gave in.

> Trust in the Lord with all thine heart; and lean not unto thine own understanding. In all thy ways acknowledge him, and he shall direct thy paths.
>
> Proverbs 3:5-6

As you can only imagine, I was troubled, and my life was out of control. I knew that I had to do something, or I was going to end up someplace I did not want to be (jail, an asylum, or dead). So, I did something I hadn't done in a long time. I prayed. I reached out and asked God for help. I also started reading the Bible (you would be surprised what you can find in that book even if you do not believe). How many of you have ever thought about reading the Bible or considered asking God for help? You know if you humbly ask for guidance and believe with all your heart and soul, He might be able to put you on the path you chose to get off long ago. He might even be able to help you with the pains, heartaches, and burdens you are suffering from. This might be the salvation you are looking for and needing in your life. Maybe, for the first time in your life, the spirit within you might be able to convince you not to give up and to continue making the right choices. All this is possible when you believe.

> And even to your old age I am he; and even to hoar hairs will I carry you: I have made, and I will bear; even I will carry, and will deliver you.
>
> Isaiah 46:4

Hopefully, there will come a time in your life when you give up your addiction and move on (the sooner the better) and you will let go of the way things used to be. When that day comes, you will begin to explore a new way of life. One that will take you places you only dreamed about. At first, you might feel alone, lost, depressed, and in despair, not knowing which way to go, but reaching out for help could be the best thing you do, so don't wait. You are going to have to believe that this path you are on is the right one.

> If any of you lack wisdom, let him ask of God, that giveth to all men liberally, and upbraideth not; and it shall be given him.
>
> James 1:5

Prepare yourself because the path you are on will be a bumpy one at first. You will be faced with things that will seem impossible to overcome. Some things might be arguments with your family and friends or disagreements with your significant other or employer, but the worst thing you might face is with yourself. Remember, you can be your worst enemy. There will be times when you want to give up and return to your old habits. Don't let this happen. Take charge and move on!

> Behold, God is my salvation; I will trust, and not be afraid: for the LORD Jehovah is my strength and my song; he also is become my salvation.
>
> Isaiah 12:2

There will also be times you are tempted, ridiculed, harassed, threatened, belittled, criticized, humiliated, shamed, rejected, and crushed by others. If that isn't bad enough, there will be people out there who want to see you fail; waiting and watching; wanting you to make that one mistake. Then out of nowhere, there they are. Telling you they "told you so," or they "knew you couldn't do it." You are going to have to avoid people like this. Don't worry about what they say or think about you. It's none of their business. Remember, this is your time to take back your life, no one else's.

"Do not think about how people see you. Instead, think about how you see yourself."

Also, watch out for demons looking like ordinary people. They are lurking all around you, preying on the weak and defenseless. You are going to have to prepare yourself by being strong, courageous, and most of all faithful, faithful to those you love and want in your life. It wouldn't hurt to keep God first on your list. It helped me.

> Behold, I send you forth as sheep in the midst of wolves:
> be ye therefore wise as serpents, and harmless as doves.
>
> Matthew 10:16

Folks, your lives can be very complicated; I know mine is. You are going to have to work on your recovery every day for the rest of your life if you want to be free from your addictions and your suffering. Giving up now is not an option; giving in could become a life sentence. It is time for all of you to search your hearts and soul for what is missing.

NOTES

_____

_____

_____

_____

_____

_____

_____

_____

_____

_____

_____

_____

_____

_____

_____

_____

_____

_____

_____

_____

_____

_____

_____

_____

_____

_____

23
You Can Do This

"Some people believe that addiction is a disease. I don't know. What I do know is that the disease started as a choice."

Your addiction! Your disease! Your choice!

What I wrote in this self-guide to recovery helped me become a better person. It can help you, too! It helped me get back to the things I needed in my life: my relationship with God; my spirituality; my family; and my friends. If I did not come up with these ideas for my recovery, I would still be fighting the demons that had a hold on me. It takes time and patience, but it works if you want it bad enough and are willing enough to try.

If you are on the same path that I was on, you will one day have to face the possibility that the path may end. You are going to have to do something now before your addiction gets worse. Take what I have written and use what works for you. There are several ideas that I discuss that will help you. I still follow my advice and have been sober for several years.

After you have read the material, picture yourself working on your recovery. Put yourself in a position that works for you. Think about ways that will overpower your behavior towards your addiction. Thinking positively about yourself and asking for God's help would be a great start!

Remember, there is more to life than your addiction. Work on making your life exciting, interesting, and fun. Try and be a part of something bigger than you are; something that can guide you to new horizons. You have to keep telling yourself you are going to make it regardless of what gets in your way, and believe me, things will get in your way. Make the right choices in your life.

I hope you noticed throughout this book that I kept mentioning "Believe in Yourself". If you don't believe in yourself, it is going to be very difficult for you to accomplish what needs to be done in your life. I strongly believe what I have put in this book will work for you. It will work if you honestly believe in yourself and want to be free from your addiction.

> For I know the thoughts that I think toward you, saith the LORD, thoughts of peace, and not of evil, to give you an expected end.
>
> Jeremiah 29:11

To God, it doesn't matter what you look like or what you wear.

It doesn't matter where you live or the places you stay.

It doesn't matter what color your skin is or the character you portray.

It doesn't matter what you did in the past or just the other day.

It doesn't matter, because God loves you just the way you are today.

God Bless

If what I have written in this book can save one life,
I have fulfilled the purpose of writing it.

NOTES

If you are having terrible thoughts about yourself, please call the Suicide and Crisis Lifeline. They provide a 24-hour service that is confidential for suicidal crises and/or emotional support.

If this is a life-threatening situation, dial 911 immediately.

Your life is worth more than you think right now. Believe me!

APPENDIX A

Al-Anon Family Groups - www.al-anon.org

Alcoholics Anonymous - www.aa.org

Celebrate Recovery - www.celebraterecovery.com

Friendship Line - www.ioaging.org/services/friendship-line

LifeRing Secular Recovery - www.lifering.org

Mental Health Hotline - www.mentalhelp.net

NAMI, National Alliance on Mental Health - www.nami.org

Home Narcotics Anonymous - www.na.org

Council of Aging - www.ncoa.org

Suicide Prevention - www.suicidepreventionlifeline.org

SAMHSA National Helpline - www.samhsa.gov

SMART Recovery - www.smartrecovery.org

Veterans Crisis Line - www.veteranscrisisline.net

SOURCES

1   TAFH, 2022, **Pain in the Nation 2022,** https://www.tfah.
    org/report-details/pain-in-the-nation-2022/
2   Yerby, Nathan, June 2022, Addiction Center, your guide for
    addiction and recovery, **Addiction Statistics**, https://www.ad-
    dictioncenter.com/addiction/addiction-statistics/